writing guides

ACTIVITIES &

Fantasy STORIES

MAGGIE LOVATT

NON-FICTION FOR AGES 9-11

Published by Scholastic Ltd,
Villiers House,
Clarendon Avenue,
Leamington Spa,
Warwickshire
CV32 5PR
Printed by Unwin Brothers Ltd,
Woking

© 2001 Scholastic Ltd
Text © 2001 Maggie Lovatt

SERIES EDITOR
Huw Thomas

AUTHOR
Maggie Lovatt

EDITOR
David Sandford

ASSISTANT EDITOR
Dulcie Booth

SERIES DESIGNER
Anna Oliwa

DESIGNER
Nari Sandhu

COVER ILLUSTRATION
Mark Oliver

ILLUSTRATIONS
Sarah Warburton

1 2 3 4 5 6 7 8 9 0   1 2 3 4 5 6 7 8 9 0

The publishers wish to thank:
The CS Lewis Company
for the use of an extract from *The
Lion, the Witch and the Wardrobe*
by CS Lewis © 1950, CS Lewis
Pte.Ltd (1950, HarperCollins
Publishers).
**The Random House Group
Limited** for the use of an extract
from *The Snow-Walker's Son* by
Catherine Fisher © 1993,
Catherine Fisher (1993, The
Bodley Head).

**Every effort has been made to
trace copyright holders and the
publishers apologise for any
omissions.**

British Library Cataloguing-in-Publication Data
A catalogue record for this book is available from the
British Library.

ISBN 0-439-01867-6

The right of Maggie Lovatt to be identified as the Author
of this work has been asserted by her in accordance
with the Copyright, Designs and Patents Act 1988.

CONTENTS

The Lion, the Witch and the Wardrobe

*I**t is raining. Lucy, Edmund, Susan and Peter have just finished breakfast and begin to explore the big house they are staying in. The first room they look in is empty except for a wardrobe. The others leave because there is nothing of interest but Lucy decides to climb in amongst the fur coats...***

Soon she went further in and found that there was a second row of coats hanging up behind the first one. It was almost quite dark in there and she kept her arms stretched out in front of her so as not to bump her face into the back of the wardrobe. She took a step further in – then two or three steps – always expecting to feel the woodwork against the tips of her fingers. But she could not feel it.

'This must be a simply enormous wardrobe!' thought Lucy, going still further in and pushing the soft folds of the coats aside to make room for her. Then she noticed that there was something crunching under her feet. 'I wonder if this is more moth-balls?' she thought, stooping down to feel it with her hand. But instead of feeling the hard, smooth wood of the floor of the wardrobe, she felt something soft and powdery and extremely cold. 'This is very queer,' she said, and went on a step or two further.

Next moment she found that what was rubbing against her face and hands was no longer soft fur but something hard and rough and even prickly. 'Why, it's just like branches of trees!' exclaimed Lucy. And then she saw that there was a light ahead of her; not a few inches away where the back of the wardrobe ought to have been, but a long way off. Something cold and soft was falling on her. A moment later she found that she was standing in the middle of a wood at night-time with snow under her feet and snowflakes falling through the air.

From *The Lion, the Witch and the Wardrobe* by CS Lewis

writing guides : FANTASY STORIES

The Snow-Walker's Son

Behind them, someone had come into the Hall, someone silent, without footsteps, someone who froze the air. Jessa felt sudden crystals harden on her face and mouth; felt a cold numbness that pierced her skin. Thorkil was still; frost glistened on his lips.

'It's Gudrun,' he breathed.

And as if the walker on the stairs had heard him, the footsteps stopped, and began to come back down.

Suddenly, Jessa had never felt so afraid. Her heart thudded; she wanted to run, had to fight to hold herself still, clenching her fingers into fists. Before them the footsteps came closer; behind in the Hall some terrible coldness loomed.

Someone was sitting in the Jarl's chair, looking no more than a bundle of rich fabrics. Then he pushed his hood back, and Jessa saw it was a very old man, thin and spry, his hair wisps of white, his look sly and sidelong.

'They leave tomorrow,' he was saying. 'As you expected.'

Astonished, Jessa stared at Thorkil.

The woman laughed, a low peal of sound that made a new surge of fear leap in Jessa's stomach.

The old man chuckled too. 'And they know all about Thrasirshall, the poor waifs.'

'What do they know?' she said.

'Oh, that the wind howls through it, that it's a wilderness of trolls and spirits on the edge of the world. Not to speak of what the Hall contains.' He spat, and then grinned.

They could just see the woman's white hands, and her sleeves. Gently, Thorkil edged the curtain a little wider.

Gudrun stood in the light from the window. She was tall and young, her skin white as a candle; her hair pure blonde and braided in long intricate braids down her back. Her ice-blue dress was edged with fur. Silver glittered at wrist and throat; she stood straight, her sharp gaze towards them. Hessa felt Thorkil's instant stillness. Even from here, they could see her eyes had no colour.

From *The Snow-Walker's Son* by Catherine Fisher

Settings: a two-world story

Real

Time

Place

Weather

Weather

Place

Time

Fantasy

Profile of a fantasy villain

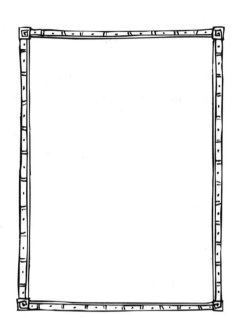

CHARACTER'S NAME:

CHARACTER'S ROLE:

OCCUPATION:
A Snow-walker (Sorceress)

AGE: SEX:

SINGLE/MARRIED:

MARRIED TO: *Jarl Ragnar*

CHILDREN:
One child, called Kari. Only seen by his mother, the midwife and his keeper Brocheal. According to the locals he is considered to be a monster and lives in exile at Thrasirshall ~ a land at the edge of the world that is cold and frozen.

PHYSICAL DESCRIPTION:

DISTINGUISHING FEATURES:

POWERS:

There are two types of fantasy stories: two-world stories, where characters move from the real world to a parallel fantasy world, as seen in The Chronicles of Narnia *by CS Lewis, or the* Harry Potter *series by JK Rowling; and one-world stories, which are set entirely in a fantasy world, for example* The Hobbit *by JRR Tolkien or* The Snow-Walker's Son *by Catherine Fisher.*

Shared activities: The Lion, the Witch and the Wardrobe

Settings – a two-world story

Read through the passage on page 4 with the children, and ask them which is the real world and which is the fantasy world. Explain that there are three aspects to settings – time, place and climate. Ask them to refer to the extract and together fill in an enlarged copy of photocopiable page 6. Explain that, typically, the real world is mundane and the fantasy world is extraordinary. Why do they think this is?

The guide

Lucy plays the role of 'guide', and we see the land of Narnia through her eyes. What would the children expect her to do as guide? (Show the reader around the different worlds, describing the people and places.) The guide is central – we are drawn into the story through their actions, reactions and descriptions. They are often a shy child who grows in confidence through the story.

Triggers

A trigger moves the guide from the real world into the fantasy world. Ask the children what the trigger is in the extract. Did Lucy know the wardrobe was magical? If she did, how would the story be different? (There would be no element of surprise.) The trigger is usually something ordinary; look at the triggers in other two-world stories, such as *Alice in Wonderland* (the rabbit hole), or *Harry Potter* (platform 9¾).

Character roles

Which typical story characters can the children find in fantasy stories? (Hero, villain, helper, guide.) Children who are familiar with *The Lion, the Witch and the Wardrobe* could suggest who fulfils each role. (Aslan, The White Witch, Mr and Mrs Beaver and Lucy respectively.) Often the guide is the central character, and could be the hero or heroine too! Together, list the qualities these characters typically possess.

Shared activities: The Snow-walker's Son

Fantasy villain

Read page 5 with the children up to *...Jessa's stomach* – can they predict which role Gudrun fulfils in this story? Read on. When do we find out what she looks like? (The last paragraph.) What impact do Jessa and Thorkil's initial reactions and observations have? Highlight these: *...someone who froze the air.* Would the last paragraph be as effective without them? Why not? (The author uses suspense to intensify our reaction to Gudrun.) Suspense hooks the reader into the story. Both extracts use another technique called a cliffhanger, where the chapter ends at a critical point. If you can, borrow a copy of either book and look at how cliffhangers work.

Descriptive language

Discuss how the author creates an image of Gudrun. Use an enlarged copy of page 7 to complete a character profile together. Encourage the children to refer to and deduce from the text. Does Gudrun have the necessary characteristics to be a villain?

writing guides: FANTASY STORIES

Looking at fantasy stories

Talk about some other fantasy stories, films or TV programmes, then complete this grid with a partner.

Fantasy story	One world or two?	Settings (there may be one or two)		Characters and their roles (hero, villain, guide)			Trigger (only used in two-world stories)	Reason for the journey or quest
The Lion, the Witch and the Wardrobe		1.	2.					
		1.	2.					
		1.	2.					
		1.	2.					

Fantasy Worlds

Fantasy-world settings

Has features from the real world which have been twisted to make them strange.

Typical characters

Fantasy stories often contain a guide, helpers, a hero, and a villain.

Fantasy creatures often feature characteristics of real-world beings.

Triggers

An object that moves the guide between the real and fantasy worlds.

Quest or Journey

Often the guide will have to overcome evil or return something to its rightful owner.

Cliffhangers

A technique used by fantasy writers to create suspense and anticipation, spurring the reader on.

Real-world Settings

A setting that will be familiar and instantly recognisable.

Problem & Resolution

In fantasy stories, there is often a battle of good over evil and a showdown between the hero and the villain.

Fantasy objects

There is often an object that has special magical powers – good or evil.

writing guides : FANTASY STORIES

Taking ideas further

So far we have identified the main features of fantasy stories: settings, triggers, character roles, suspense and descriptive language. The following activities will look at other features that are also essential components of fantasy stories.

As a class, brainstorm the titles of fantasy stories, films or TV programmes with which the children are familiar. Write the suggestions on the board then, as a class or in pairs complete an enlarged copy of photocopiable page 9, identifying the features of some of the children's favourite fantasy stories.

Photocopiable page 10 provides a poster that can be enlarged and used as an overview of the features of fantasy stories when discussing the following activities with the children.

Quests

All fantasy stories contain some form of quest that carries the guide on a journey through the story and gives the story a purpose. Often the task is not immediately apparent and the guide may not initially be willing to do it. Four types of quest can be identified in fantasy stories: to claim, to fight, to find, and to overcome. There is often a journey and a series of tests or challenges involved in the quest – which is where the helpers come in. These typically end with a battle between the guide and/ or fantasy hero and the fantasy villain. Can the children suggest what the quests or challenges are in some fantasy stories they know?

In *The Lion, the Witch and the Wardrobe* the children's quest is to overcome the White Witch and free Narnia of its everlasting winter. If possible, watch the video of *The Lion, the Witch and the Wardrobe* (BBC Video, BBCV5564) as a class and list the challenges the children face during their quest to free Narnia.

Fantasy objects

Recap on how the reader is drawn into a fantasy world, and how the glimpses of 'normality' make the bizarre features of the fantasy world more believable. Fantasy objects are often recognisable everyday objects that have been made fantastical by lacing them with magical powers. Can the children make a list of fantasy objects they know of from stories they have read (for example, from the *Harry Potter* series)?

What makes a fantasy world?

Reflect on the fantasy worlds described in the two extracts on pages 4 and 5. Notice how they both maintain a degree of 'normality', or have similarities with our own world. These traces of normality are 'hooks' that the reader is able to latch on to so they can be 'drawn in' to the fantasy world. In fantasy worlds virtually anything can be accepted, but although the world may be very different it will still include routines, social codes and human functions to which we can relate. If a fantasy world was void of anything we could relate to, the reader would find it very difficult to make sense of it and therefore to believe in its existence.

Extension ideas

● Ask the class to bring in from home some fantasy books they have read. Can they identify some of the features discussed and locate them in the book with Post-it notes? Many popular fantasy stories have websites which children could visit to find out more about the stories, such as the Narnia website (www.narnia.com), where children can take a tour of the land of Narnia.

● Compare film productions of fantasy stories with their book versions, for example *The Lion, the Witch and the Wardrobe* or *The Never-Ending Story*.

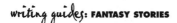 *writing guides:* **FANTASY STORIES**

So far, in Section One, children have been introduced to the characteristic features of fantasy stories and have explored how these reveal themselves in a number of fantasy contexts. They should now be ready to move on to developing some of these features themselves in preparation for writing their own fantasy story later on.

Planning

One of the first activities children will undertake when writing their extended story will be to make a plan, incorporating a clear plot structure, main characters and key events. The work in this section will provide them with resource material to help them make these initial decisions; it will also support them as they write and as their story develops a life of its own – sometimes demanding new ideas not included in the initial plan.

Photocopiable page 17 recaps the main character types and can be used for later planning support. Further Section Two activities focus on creating ideas for the other components of a fantasy story: developing the character of the 'guide'; coming up with ideas for triggers – objects that enable the guide to move between the real and the fantasy worlds; and creating fantasy settings, fantasy characters and fantasy creatures.

Using imagination

The children should be reminded that in most cases their fantasy story will be more believable if it is based on something in the real world. However, the aim is not just to tweak reality – encourage the children to let their imaginations take off. They should try to invent settings and characters that are truly fantastical, maybe even bizarre; this will not prevent these characters from doing relatively ordinary things such as having tea or playing a musical instrument, as the characters in Narnia do. Indeed, the combination of the extraordinary and the ordinary can be very persuasive.

The more imaginative the children's work is in Section Two, the more ideas they will have to feed into the extended story they are going to write as a project in Section Three.

WHO AM I?
WHAT YOU NEED
Copies of photocopiable page 17, pencils, the list of character roles generated in Section One.

WHAT TO DO
Recap with the children the different character roles found in fantasy stories. Briefly discuss the characteristics you would expect each character to possess, such as a fantasy hero being brave for example.

Give each pair of children a copy of photocopiable page 17. They should cut out the character cards, separating the roles from the descriptions. Ask them to lay the cards face-up, carefully read through the descriptions and try to match them to the character roles. In their pairs, they should discuss what other traits these characters might have. Tell them that 'good' and 'evil' are both traits, and they should add one of these, as well as any other extra facts they can think of, in the space provided on the description card. On the back of the role cards the children can write some of the names of characters from fantasy stories they know or have discussed.

Extend the activity by asking the children if they think there are any other character roles that could be found in fantasy stories. They could add their own suggested roles and description to the pack of cards for other pairs to match up. Keep the children's sets of completed character cards for use in other activities.

FANTASY TRIGGERS
WHAT YOU NEED
Copies of photocopiable page 18, writing materials.

WHAT TO DO
Recap with the class on what makes a fantasy trigger: an object that allows characters to be transported from the real world to the fantasy world and back again. Recall the examples discussed in Section One, noting how the triggers are often part of the real-world surroundings (for example, the wardrobe from *The Lion, the Witch and the Wardrobe*). Say that there could be a fantasy trigger in the classroom – can the children suggest what the object might be? How might it work?

Give each child a copy of photocopiable page 18, and explain that they should study the real- and fantasy-world situations on the sheet, creating suitable triggers that would move the characters between the two worlds. Write the name of the object and notes on how it works in the space in the middle.

CREATING FANTASY WORLDS
WHAT YOU NEED
A picture of a classroom or other familiar setting, a whiteboard or large sheet of paper, a marker pen, copies of photocopiable page 19, writing materials, paper.

WHAT TO DO
Show the children the picture of a real-world setting, and ask them whether they think it is from a real or a fantasy world. Typical responses will be that the classroom is set in the real world because it contains objects, equipment and furniture that is similar to what they can see around them. Next, recall how fantasy writers ensure that their fantasy worlds have some similarities to the real world so that the reader can 'latch on' to these features and therefore believe in the fantasy world. Remind

the children that while features of the real world are included in the fantasy world they are often twisted or changed in quite impossible ways. Ask them to consider how the classroom could be altered to persuade an onlooker that it is not real but part of a fantasy world (for example, giant tables, tiny children, books that fly and so on). Make a list of the children's ideas on the board with descriptions and sketches to explain the changes.

Provide each child with a copy of photocopiable page 19. Working in small groups, tell them to discuss ways of changing the features of the 'real' settings on the sheet in order to create a fantasy world. They should write notes in the boxes on the right of the sheet, and it may help if they draw individual sketches on a separate sheet of paper to aid their explanations. Remind the children that they should keep a few of the features from the real world so that the reader can make sense of the fantasy world.

BEWARE OF THE FANTASY VILLAIN

WHAT YOU NEED

A board or flip chart, completed copies of photocopiable page 19, large sheets of paper, writing and drawing materials.

WHAT TO DO

Tell the class that they are going to create a fantasy villain for one of the fantasy worlds they imagined in the previous activity. Ask the children to recap on what the typical characteristics of a fantasy villain are (controls or partially controls the fantasy world; is very powerful; is probably evil). Note these on the board, then brainstorm what other characteristics they may have. Might they have fearsome looks? Physical strength? Where would they live? How might they move around their world?

Ask the children to work in pairs. Using their completed copies of photocopiable page 19 from the previous activity, they should choose a fantasy world and then design a fantasy villain to live in it. They should draw their villain in the middle of a large sheet of paper and make notes all around about the characteristics their villain has (such as where they live, and how they move, fight and so on). Encourage them to make sure that there are links with the special nature of the fantasy world in which they live.

Extend the activity by asking children to write a job advertisement for the local paper, advertising for someone to be their fantasy villain.

OBJECTIVE

■ To create a fantasy villain for a fantasy world.

THE GUIDE

WHAT YOU NEED

Copies of photocopiable page 20, writing and drawing materials, completed copies of photocopiable page 19, the completed character cards from the 'Who am I?' activity (photocopiable page 17).

WHAT TO DO

Recap on the character roles found in fantasy texts, this time focusing on the guide and reflecting on their role in the story. Ask the children to refer back to the character cards they created in the 'Who am I?' activity, and to share the extra facts they wrote on their cards for the guide character. Confirm that the guide is central to the story, as it is through their eyes that we learn about the fantasy world; note also that the guide is often fairly ordinary, making it easier for the reader to relate to them. Can the children offer examples of guides from their own reading?

OBJECTIVE

■ To create a guide for a fantasy world.

Provide a copy of photocopiable page 20 for each child. Explain that they should choose one of the fantasy worlds they created on photocopiable page 19, and a fantasy villain from the previous activity. Using the characteristics from the guide's character card as a reminder, they should go on to imagine a guide to visit their fantasy world and complete their own profile for him or her.

SETTING A CHALLENGE

WHAT YOU NEED
Large (A2) sheets of paper, marker pens.

OBJECTIVE
■ To devise a series of quests to be used in fantasy stories.

WHAT TO DO
Emphasise that in fantasy stories the guide will, at some point, be faced with a quest or challenge, and that this will entail some form of journey and a battle of good versus evil. Can the class remember the four different types of quests outlined in Section One?

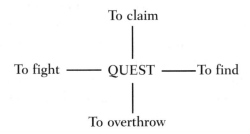

Draw the above web on the board, then divide the class into groups of four. Give each group a large sheet of paper and a selection of marker pens and ask them to copy the web onto their piece of paper. Ask them to discuss ideas for each of the four types of quest and to write examples by each name. Encourage them to write down their ideas even if they are unsure whether or not they will work in a story. Finally, as a class, share all the ideas and save them for future reference.

FANTASTIC OBJECTS

WHAT YOU NEED
The list of fantasy objects created in Section One, a selection of everyday objects (such as an umbrella, a pair of shoes, a large bag, a key, and so on) enough for one between two, copies of photocopiable page 21, writing materials, timer.

OBJECTIVES
■ To draw the reader into a fantasy world through the eyes of the guide.
■ To create fantasy objects.

WHAT TO DO
Remind the class that the guide encounters many different things in the fantasy world – fantasy heroes, villains, creatures and objects – and that it is the guide who explains these features to the reader. Refer back to the list of fantasy objects made in Section One to jog the children's memories, and note how the objects are recognisable but made special because of the particular powers they have.

Ask the children to work in pairs; give each pair an everyday object and explain that they will have five minutes to discuss the following:
● What special powers they would give to their everyday object to transform it into a fantasy object.
● What they would be able to do with the object in the fantasy world that they wouldn't be able to do in the real world.
● After five minutes ask the pairs to act as guides and explain their fantasy objects to the class.

● Give each child a copy of photocopiable page 21. Ask them to look at the objects listed, and to discuss how they would change each one into a fantasy object, explaining its special powers and what it does in the fantasy world.

FANTASY CREATURES CATALOGUE
WHAT YOU NEED

Large sheets of paper, strips of paper approximately 10cm x 25cm (folded in half widthways), writing and drawing materials, display space, the list of examples of fantasy creatures from Section One.

WHAT TO DO

Discuss with the children what makes a fantasy creature. Confirm that they are based on something we are familiar with, but that has been altered to create something new and fantastic. With this definition in mind, ask the children to work in groups and to brainstorm all the fantastic creatures they know (from books, films, general knowledge, games and so on), listing them on a large sheet of paper. They should then each choose a creature from their list and draw a picture of it on one half of a strip of paper. On the other half they should make notes about it, such as its name, where it would be found, what it does, whether it is scary or friendly.

When they have finished, make a 'Fantasy creatures catalogue': display all the children's fantasy creatures in alphabetical order on the back of the classroom door, on a washing line or in the form of a book so that the children can use them as a reference source later.

MY OWN FANTASY CREATURE
WHAT YOU NEED

The 'Fantasy creatures catalogue' from the previous activity, copies of photocopiable page 22, writing and drawing materials.

WHAT TO DO

Ask the class to pick out their favourite fantasy creatures from the class collection. Discuss the children's choices, considering what makes them believable and fantastic. For example, are they made up of a combination of recognisable features from humans and other animals? What are the weirdest animals? Why?

Give each child a copy of photocopiable page 22. Explain that they should choose an animal from the real world and alter it to create a fantasy creature. Ask them to draw a labelled picture of their fantasy creature in the space on the photocopiable sheet, and then to describe it from the point of view of the guide. Encourage them to imagine they are the guide seeing the creature for the first time, and to include vivid adjectives, metaphors and similes to bring the creature to life for the reader, rather than simple, flat, matter-of-fact descriptions.

Who am I?

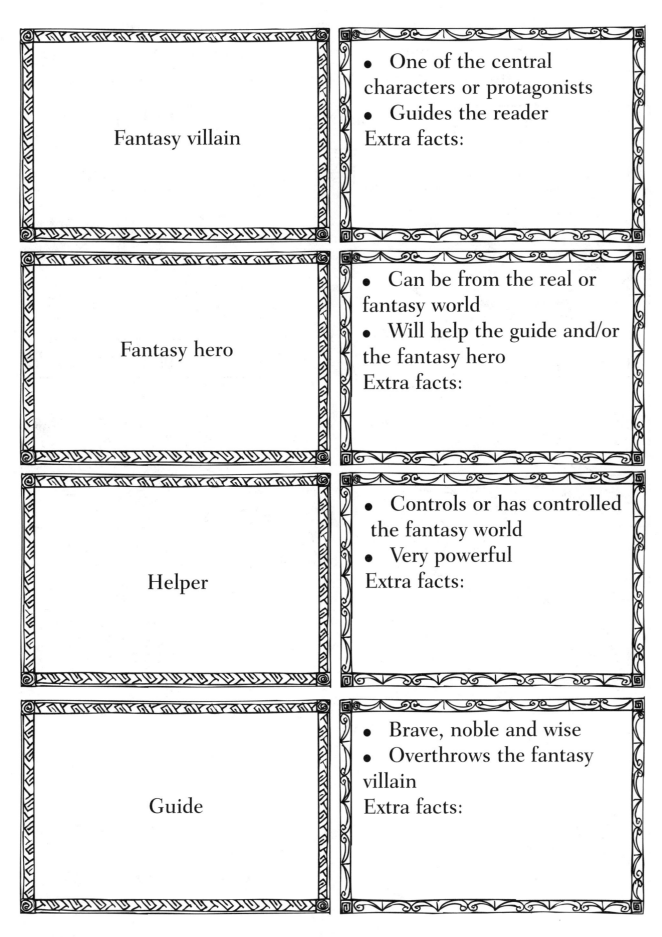

Fantasy villain

- One of the central characters or protagonists
- Guides the reader

Extra facts:

Fantasy hero

- Can be from the real or fantasy world
- Will help the guide and/or the fantasy hero

Extra facts:

Helper

- Controls or has controlled the fantasy world
- Very powerful

Extra facts:

Guide

- Brave, noble and wise
- Overthrows the fantasy villain

Extra facts:

writing guides: **FANTASY STORIES**

Fantasy triggers

Look at the four real-world settings below. Think of a different trigger to take you from each place to its fantasy-world partner. Remember that your trigger needs to be part of the real world.

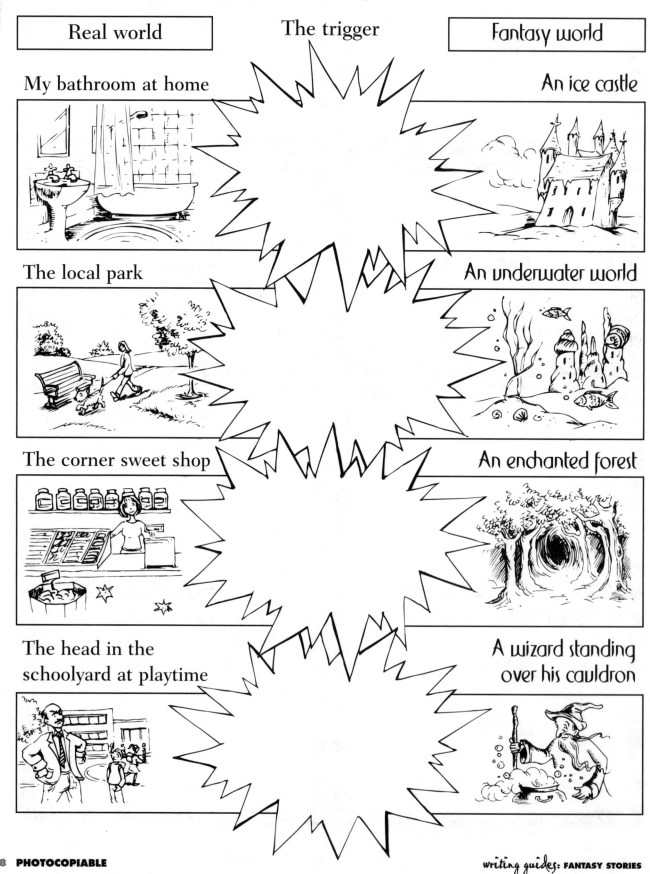

| Real world | The trigger | Fantasy world |

My bathroom at home — **An ice castle**

The local park — **An underwater world**

The corner sweet shop — **An enchanted forest**

The head in the schoolyard at playtime — **A wizard standing over his cauldron**

writing guides: **FANTASY STORIES**

Creating fantasy worlds

Think about these real-world settings. How would you change each one to make it into a fantasy world? Note the changes you would make in the space on the right.

Real world   Changes

The guide

Choose one of the fantasy worlds you have created, and write the profile of a guide to take you through it below.

Describe your fantasy world:

The fantasy villain is:

Picture of guide:

Front   Side view

Distinguishing features:

Name: Age:

Significant facts about him/her: (Any connections with the fantasy villain?)

Important strengths/ qualities they will bring to their job:

Fantasy objects

See if you can change the everyday objects below into fantasy objects.
Write your explanations of what they do on the labels underneath.

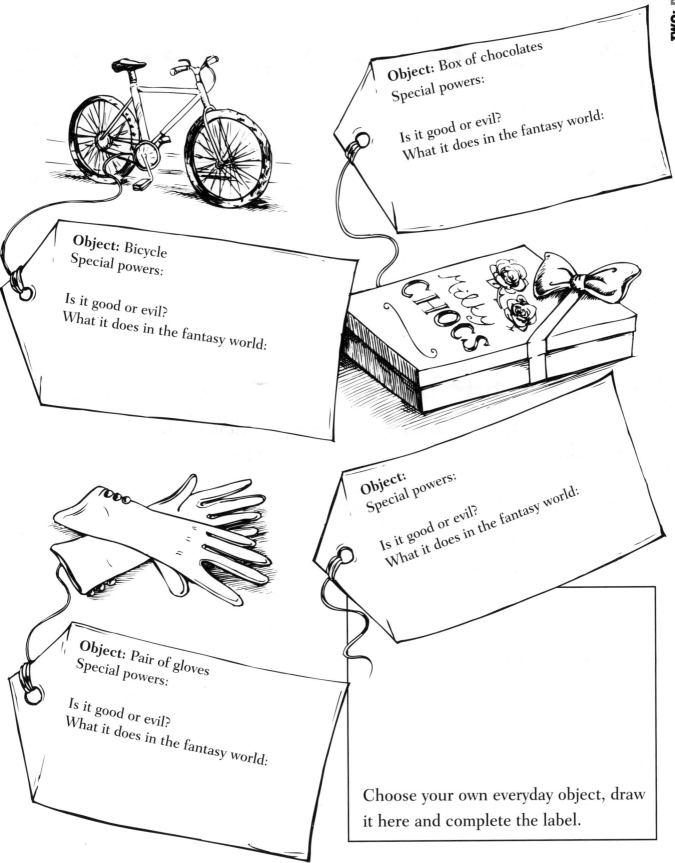

Object: Box of chocolates
Special powers:

Is it good or evil?
What it does in the fantasy world:

Object: Bicycle
Special powers:

Is it good or evil?
What it does in the fantasy world:

Object:
Special powers:

Is it good or evil?
What it does in the fantasy world:

Object: Pair of gloves
Special powers:

Is it good or evil?
What it does in the fantasy world:

Choose your own everyday object, draw
it here and complete the label.

writing guides: **FANTASY STORIES**

Fantasy creature

Invent your own fantasy creature. Base it on a real-world creature, then give it fantastic features.

Draw a labelled picture of your creature in the box.

Now describe your creature from the point of view of the guide. Make it come alive using adjectives, metaphors and similes.

I saw the creature for the first time. It was extraordinary

_____

_____

_____

_____

_____

_____

_____

_____

_____

_____

writing guides: **FANTASY STORIES**

Now is the chance to put everything the children have learned about fantasy stories into practice! This section will provide you with ideas on how to develop the children's fantasy-story writing techniques. The ideas are based on what has been learned in Sections One and Two, and all the writing activities can be modelled as shared writing and/or supported as guided writing. It is advisable that the children have access to their work from Section Two, as well as the reference poster and comparative 'Looking at fantasy stories' chart from Section One.

A fantasy story project

The story planner on pages 26–7 can form the basis of an extended piece of work into which children can incorporate some or all of the other activities in Section Three. Together, they provide an opportunity to plan and write a complete fantasy story using many of the features identified and explored in Sections One and Two. Once the plan is completed, the children can go on to draft, edit, revise and produce a final version of their story. Any of the other activities in this section can be used to develop individual aspects of the story.

This will be an extensive writing project and it is important to set the children interim targets as well as monitoring, discussing and offering feedback on how their stories are developing. You might like to set up pairs of 'author partners' with whom children spend ten minutes each session, discussing and editing their work so far. Once the stories are complete, children can illustrate them and design a front and back cover for their story. Encourage them to look at a range of fantasy books to get a feel for typical cover styles. They could write a blurb and ask their author partner to write a brief review for inclusion on the back cover.

Notes for an opening chapter

Photocopiable page 25 will help children to structure and write the opening chapter for a two-world fantasy story. You may prefer to use this activity after the children have completed the first draft of their story plan using pages 26–7, drawing on the decisions they have made there. Tell them to set the scene and introduce the guide character in the real world where everything is normal. They should then explain how the guide discovers the trigger and how it moves him or her into the fantasy world. Encourage them to refer back to their completed worksheets from Section Two for ideas. The work done by less able children on this activity may form their complete opening chapter; more able children may just make notes that they can develop more fully elsewhere.

Story planner

This planner on photocopiable pages 26–7 is designed to support children in writing their own complete one- or two-world fantasy story. (If they choose to write a one-world fantasy story they will not need to fill in the marked sections.) Encourage the children to make notes under each of the headings, referring back to the ideas they came up with in Section Two to help them. Once they start writing their story, they may think of new ideas or want to add details and make changes. Encourage them to use the plan as a working document on which to make notes and jot down ideas to help them during their writing.

Tell the children to use their imagination to create a world and characters that the reader can believe in and can 'see' in their mind's eye. Remind them that their fantasy world should be coherent and that there should be connections between the things within it (creatures, villains, the hero, fantasy objects, and so on). For

THREE: WRITING

example, the quest or challenge is often created by the villain; fantasy creatures can be good or evil and one of them could be a friend to the guide while others may be on the side of the villain.

A map

Many fantasy stories have a map of the fantasy world in which they are set at the beginning of the book, so the reader can refer to and trace the journey taken by the guide through the world. Drawing a map of their fantasy world will help children develop their story coherently. Encourage them to include at least five locations, one of which should be the home of the fantasy villain

The challenge or quest

Drawing a map may help children to decide upon an appropriate quest for their story (look back at the quest brainstorms created in Section Two for more ideas), and to anticipate where challenges or tests may arise during the journey. Photocopiable page 28 will help children to put their thoughts about these challenges down on paper – maybe the guide has to find a secret route through a mountain to find a key, or pass a fierce fantasy creature. At the same time, children can consider who might help them and what fantasy objects they could use.

Building up tension

Use photocopiable page 29 to help children to build up tension in advance of an event being described. Remind them of Jessa and Thorkil's first glimpse of Gudrun from *The Snow-Walker's Son*, and how the author used suspense to increase the impact of Gudrun's appearance on the reader: we were told how Jessa and Thorkil felt before we were told what Gudrun looked like. Explain to the children that you would like them to adopt this technique before introducing the fantasy villain into their story, building up fear and keeping the reader in suspense. They should try to describe the moment in which the guide meets the villain without saying what the villain looks like.

Invite children to picture the fantasy villain in their head (this may be the one they invented in 'Fantasy creatures' on page 22, or a new one). Tell them to imagine they are the guide and to make notes on a copy of page 29. They should describe the scene, building up an atmosphere of fear. It may be a dark wood, a high mountain, a castle or another building. They should then describe the impact the villain has on the guide before saying what he or she looks like and before the two meet.

24 **TEACHER'S NOTES**

writing guides: **FANTASY STORIES**

Notes for an opening chapter

Use these headings to plan the opening chapter of your fantasy story.

Set the scene in the real world and introduce your guide.

A trigger moves the guide into the fantasy world. What happens?

Now the guide is in the fantasy world, what do they see, feel, smell, hear?

End your chapter with a cliffhanger...

writing guides: **FANTASY STORIES**

Story plan

Use this page to plan the parts of your fantasy story and make notes about any changes you would like to make to your story drafts

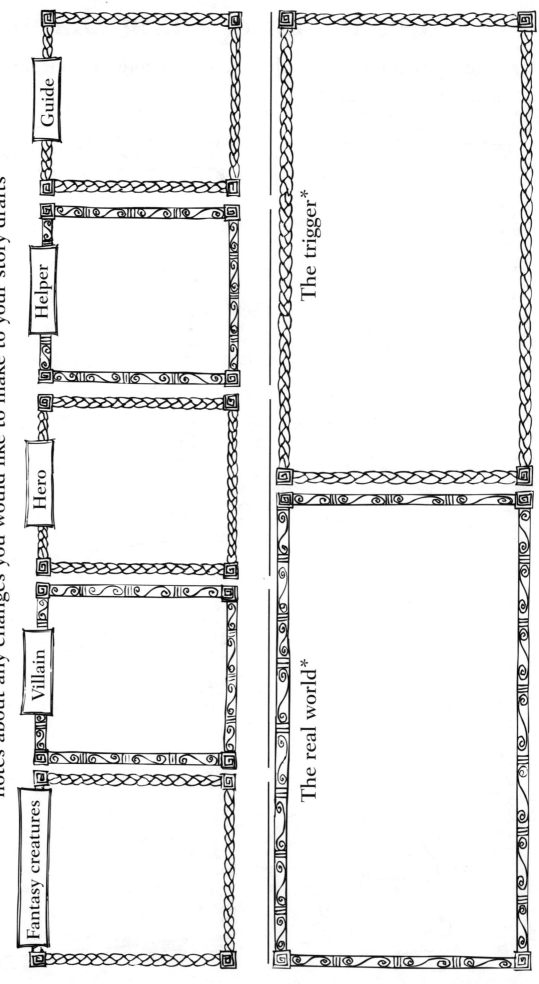

Fantasy creatures

Villain

Hero

Helper

Guide

The real world*

The trigger*

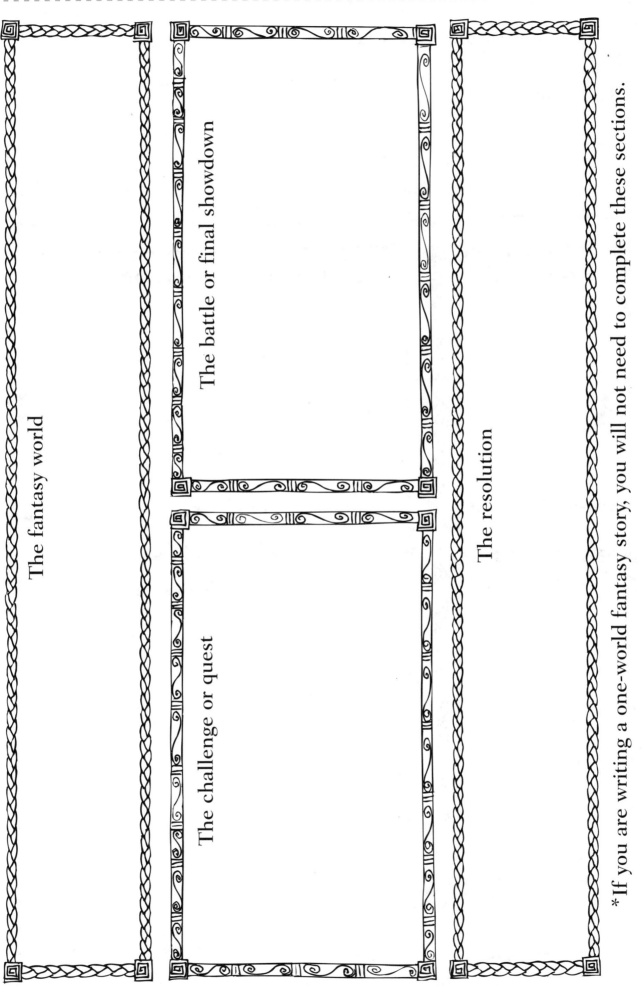

The fantasy world

The battle or final showdown

The challenge or quest

The resolution

*If you are writing a one-world fantasy story, you will not need to complete these sections.

writing guides: **FANTASY STORIES**

The challenge or quest

The challenge or quest

First obstacle

How the guide overcame it

Second obstacle

How the guide overcame it

Fantasy objects used

writing guides: **FANTASY STORIES**

Building up tension

Describe the moment when the guide meets the villain.
Don't say what the villain looks like!

 What has the guide been told about the fantasy villain? (Make the reader feel nervous.)

 Where does the guide meet the villain? (Make the reader feel uncomfortable.)

Is it dark or light?

Is it windy or rainy?

Is it hot or cold?

Are there shadows?

 When the guide sees the villain from a distance... (Don't say what the villain looks like!)

What do they think?

What do they feel?

What do they notice first? (A smell, a sound, a movement.)

 What is the villain doing? How are they moving? Is there a noise or smell?

 How does the guide read?

How do they move? (Quickly? Slowly?)

Do they make any noise?

What do they do? (Hide? Run? Approach? Speak?)

The objectives of the work the children have completed so far in Sections One, Two and Three have been:
- *to identify the generic features of fantasy stories*
- *to explore and compare these features by looking at examples in texts, TV, films, and so on*
- *to write examples of the features identified*
- *to write an extended fantasy story that incorporates several typical features. This section aims to encourage children to look critically at their work, comparing it with these features of fantasy stories, and making suggestions for improvements to their own and others' work.*

Fantasy review

When reviewing the writing produced in Section Three, it is important to evaluate how effectively the features of fantasy stories that were identified in Sections One and Two have been incorporated, and whether they have been included appropriately as opposed to simply ticking off those that have been included. For example, a trigger may be included in the children's story, but it should only be included in a two-world fantasy story and should be an inconspicuous object in the real world.

Photocopiable page 31 provides a checklist of fantasy story features for children to use when reviewing their own work. Encourage them to be critical when re-reading their work, and to use the checklist to decide on any improvements they might like to make to their story.

Guiding struggling writers

For less able children, ask them to tackle one section only of the writing project. Focus on limited features (such as writing an opening chapter and developing the character of the guide), and encourage them to make use of the story-planning activities in Section Three to provide a framework for them to build their story around. You could appoint a 'mentor' from within the class or from the year above to guide, help and inspire, writing positive reviews of the children's work to be displayed alongside it; or pair children to work together on a story, so they can share ideas and support one another when working.

The comment cards on page 32 can be used and adapted by either mentors or writing partners in order to give clear feedback and set targets for improvement when developing a fantasy story.

Author circles

'Author circles' provide children with the opportunity to share their work, to inspire others, raise expectations, reinforce learning objectives and develop the ability to give constructive feedback. To focus discussion, provide each child with a set of feedback cards listing some features of fantasy stories from photocopiable page 32. Working in groups of similar ability, the children should read photocopies of one another's work (so that everyone in the circle has a copy), and fill out comment cards to attach to the relevant parts of the work as prompts for discussion of the work. Ensure that any feedback is positive!

 # Fantasy review

Name:		Fantasy story:	✓
Character roles	Guide	Is the guide a fairly ordinary child? Does he or she draw the reader into the story, showing us what they encounter in a variety of ways, such as description, reaction, explanation, stories within stories?	☐
	Hero	Is the character brave, noble, wise, and good? Do they successfully overthrow the fantasy villain?	☐
	Villain	Is the character evil? Powerful? Does he or she control the fantasy world or possess magical powers?	☐
	Helpers	These can be from the real or fantasy world. They will be fairly low key. Do they help the guide and/or fantasy hero?	☐
Fantasy creatures		Are they based on something familiar? Have they been altered to make something new and fantastic?	☐
Fantasy objects		Are these convincing? Do they possess magical powers?	☐
The quest	The quest or challenge	Does this tie up with the problem created by the fantasy villain? The quest usually aims to overthrow the villain's reign.	☐
	Obstacles or tests	Are these convincing? Are the tasks in keeping with the fantasy world?	☐
	Resolution	Does good champion over evil? Is the world released from the villain's power? Is the villain eradicated or simply weakened (leaving the potential for a sequel)?	☐
Trigger		Is this something familiar in the real world, but not glaringly obvious?	☐
Settings	Real	Is this ordinary and instantly recognisable?	☐
	Fantasy	Can the reader make sense of the world? Does it contain traces of normality, which the reader can latch on to?	☐
Suspense	Cliffhangers	Do they add suspense? Do they leave the reader wanting to read on?	☐
	Build-up	Does this lead the reader to think the worst?	☐
Descriptive language		Have adjectives, verbs and adverbs been carefully chosen to create images in the reader's mind?	☐

Comment cards

Fantasy-world setting
I like the way you

You could improve this
feature by

The guide
I though it was great when you

This would work even better if

Your description of
was great.

This could work even better if

Real-world setting
I like the way you

You could improve this
feature by

The villain
I though it was great when you

This would work even better if

Your description of
was great.

This could work even better if

The trigger
I like the way you

You could improve this
feature by

The hero
I thought it was great when you

This would work even better if

The suspense was good when you

You could introduce even more
suspense when

writing guides: **FANTASY STORIES**